Mortimer's Fun with Words

Ending Letters

Karen Bryant-Mole

Gareth Stevens Publishing
A WORLD ALMANAC EDUCATION GROUP COMPANY

Mortimer's Fun with Words

For a free color catalog describing Gareth Stevens' list of high-quality books and multimedia programs, call 1-800-542-2595 (USA) or 1-800-461-9120 (Canada). Gareth Stevens Publishing's Fax: (414) 332-3567.

Library of Congress Cataloging-in-Publication Data available upon request from publisher. Fax: (414) 332-3567 for the attention of the Publishing Records Department.

ISBN 0-8368-2747-3

This North American edition first published in 2000 by
Gareth Stevens Publishing
A World Almanac Education Group Company
330 West Olive Street, Suite 100
Milwaukee, WI 53212 USA

This edition © 2000 by Gareth Stevens, Inc. Original © BryantMole Books, 1999. First published in 1999 by Evans Brothers Limited, 2A Portman Mansions, Chiltern Street, London W1M 1LE, United Kingdom. Additional end matter © 2000 by Gareth Stevens, Inc.

Created by Karen Bryant-Mole
Photographs by Zul Mukhida
Designed by Jean Wheeler
Teddy bear by Merrythought Ltd.

Printed in the United States of America

1 2 3 4 5 6 7 8 9 04 03 02 01 00

contents

...nt

Mortimer is going to water a plant.

The word **plant** ends with the letters **nt**.

Say the names of
these animals.

Which one ends with
the letters **nt**?

Mortimer is wearing a kilt.

The word **kilt** ends with the letters **lt**.

Here are other things you can wear.

Which one ends with
the letters **lt**?

...st

Mortimer is hungry for toast.

The word **toast** ends with the letters **st**.

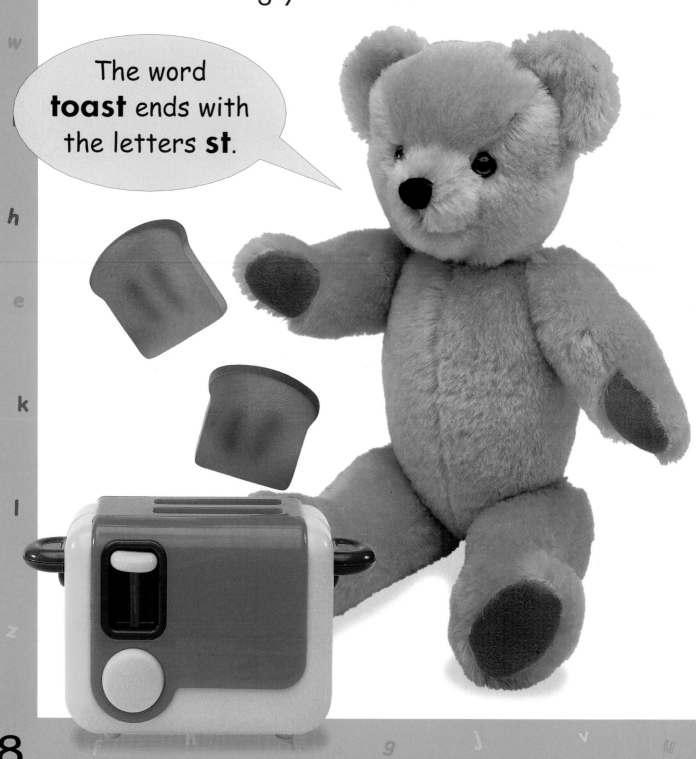

Name these animal homes.

Which one ends with
the letters **st**?

...sk

Mortimer is hiding behind a party mask.

The word **mask** ends with the letters **sk**.

You might use these things
to cook in the kitchen.

Which one ends
with the letters **sk**?

...nk

Mortimer is having something to drink.

The word **drink** ends with the letters **nk**.

Here are some colored markers.
Say the name of each color.
Which one ends with
the letters **nk**?

...lk

Mortimer's tie is made of silk.

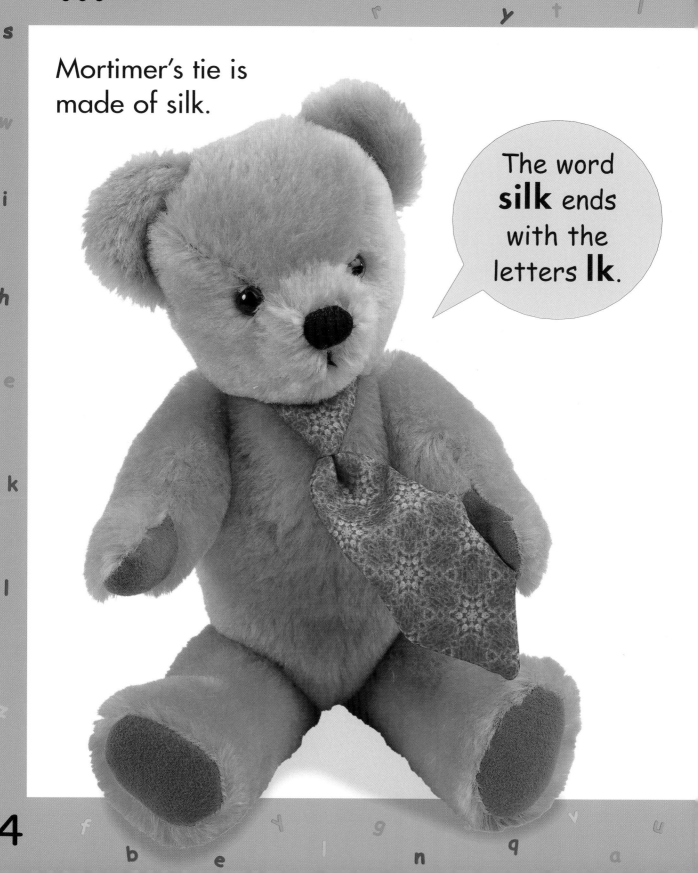

The word **silk** ends with the letters **lk**.

Here are foods
you can buy at
the supermarket.

Which food ends
with the letters **lk**?

...lf

Mortimer's clock is on a shelf.

The word **shelf** ends with the letters **lf**.

Here are some things you can use to play sports.

Which sport ends with the letters **lf**?

Mortimer put a stamp on the envelope.

The word **stamp** ends with the letters **mp**.

You might find these
things in your house.

Which one ends with
the letters **mp**?

...nd

Mortimer is playing in the sand.

The word **sand** ends with the letters **nd**.

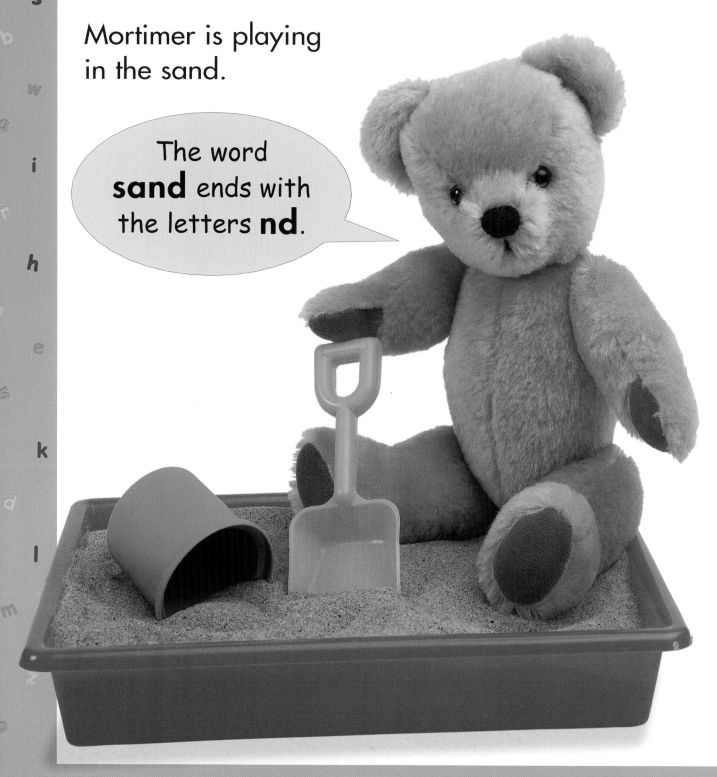

Here are some toys that look like parts of your body.

Which part ends with the letters **nd**?

...ng

Mortimer is dressed like a king.

The word **king** ends with the letters **ng**.

Here are a few pieces of jewelry.

Which piece ends with the letters **ng**?

glossary/index

envelope — a flat paper wrapper that is used to hold a card or letter 18

jewelry — decorations that are worn, such as rings, necklaces, or earrings 23

kilt — a skirt with pleats, or folds, that is often made of wool; kilts are worn by men in Scotland 6

king — a man who rules a country 22

markers — tools used for writing or drawing, which often have soft tips and colorful shades of ink 13

mask — a cover that hides the face and is worn to pretend to be someone or something else 10

shelf — a piece of furniture that is used to hold things, such as books 16

silk — soft, smooth, and shiny material 14

tie — a narrow piece of clothing that is worn around the neck 14

videos

Clifford's Fun with Sounds. (Family Home Entertainment)

Letter Fun. (Tapeworm)

Phonics and Fables. (Quality Time Education, Inc.)